THIS BOOK
BELONGS TO:

I spy with my little eye
Something beginning with ...

It's an

Apple

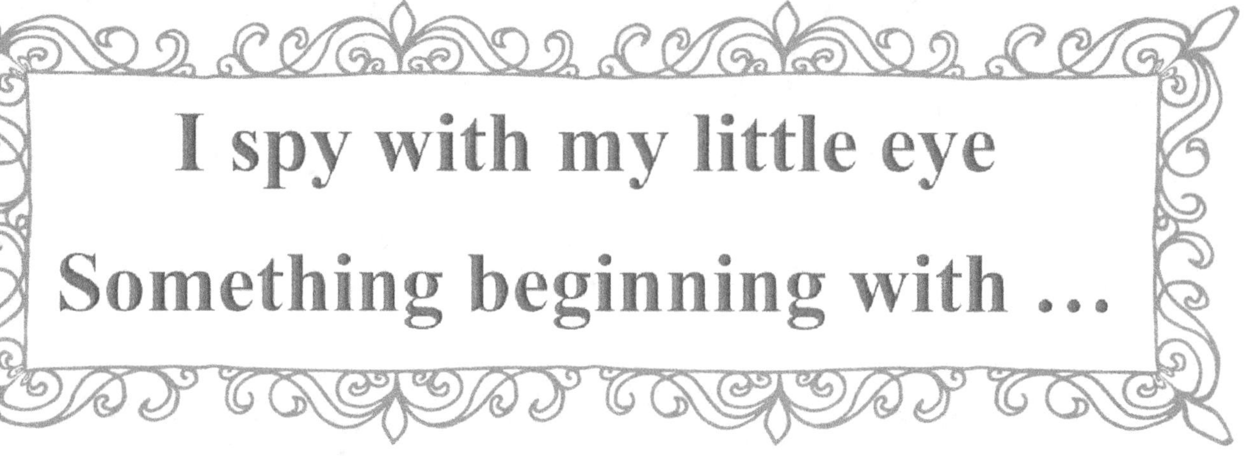

B

It's a

Bouquet

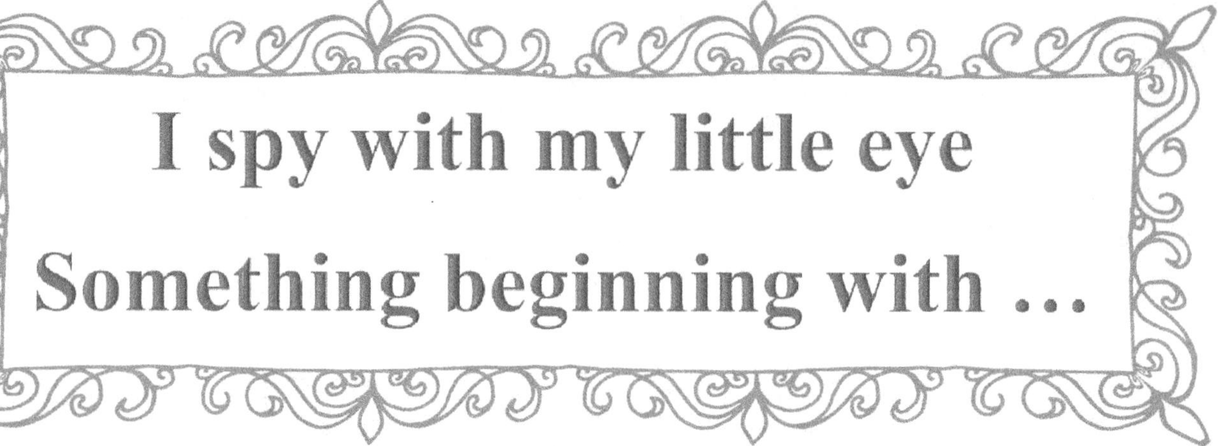

I spy with my little eye
Something beginning with …

C

It's a

Corn

I spy with my little eye
Something beginning with …

It's a

Dish

I spy with my little eye
Something beginning with …

It's an

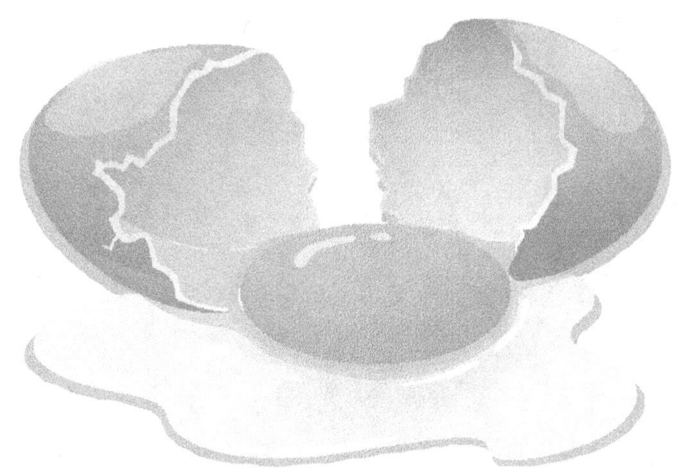

Egg

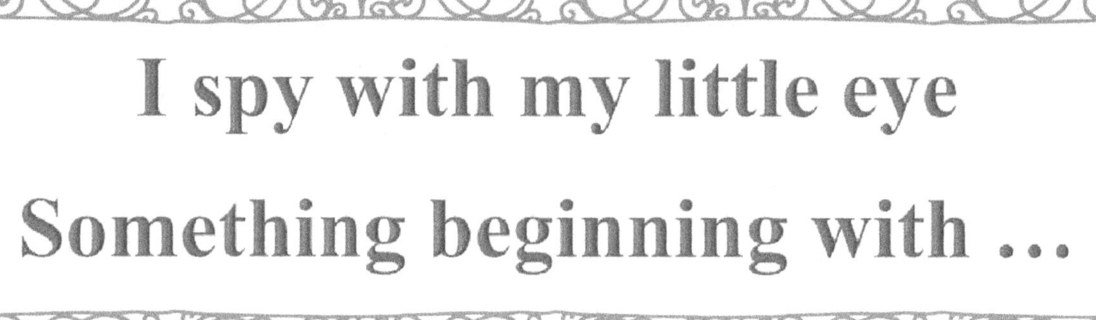

F

It's a

Flower

I spy with my little eye
Something beginning with ...

It's a

Goose

I spy with my little eye

Something beginning with …

H

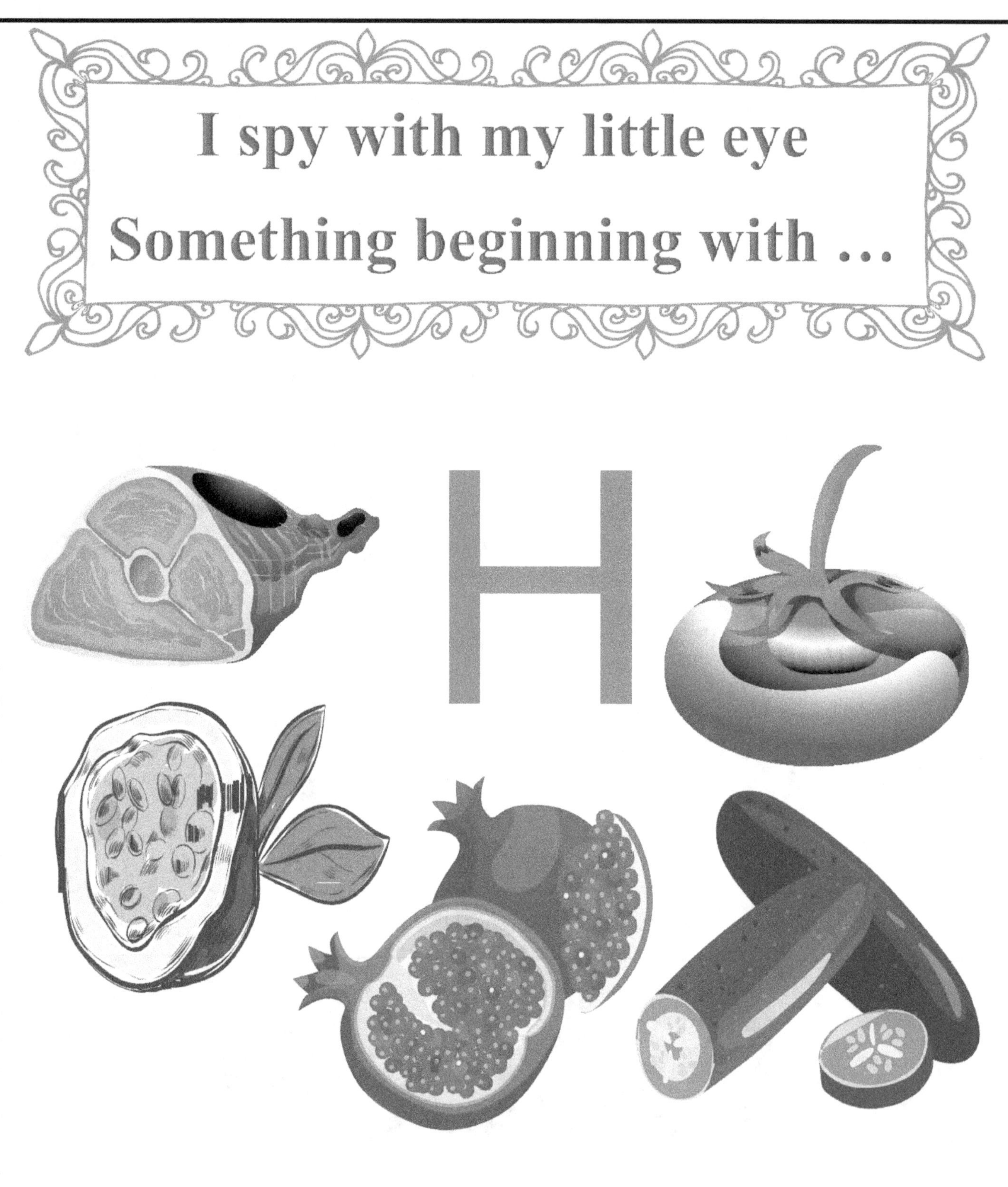

It's

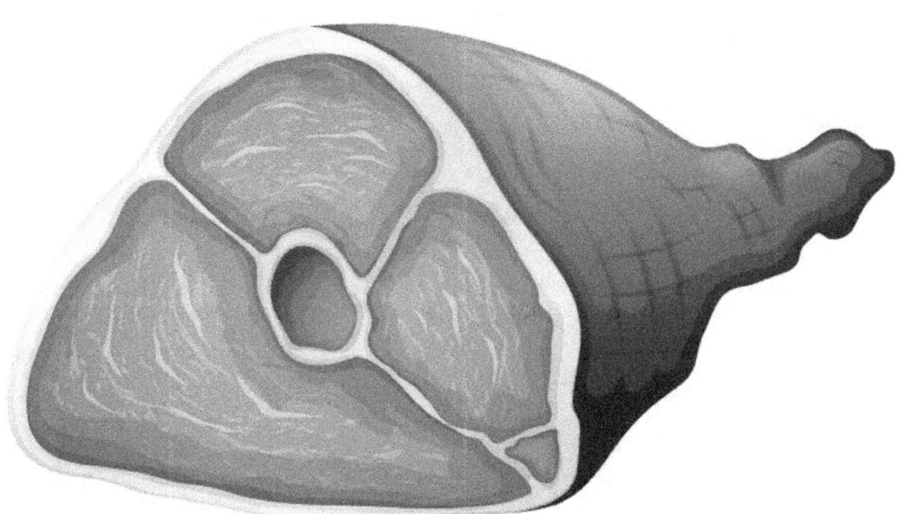

Ham

I spy with my little eye
Something beginning with …

It's an

Ice Cream

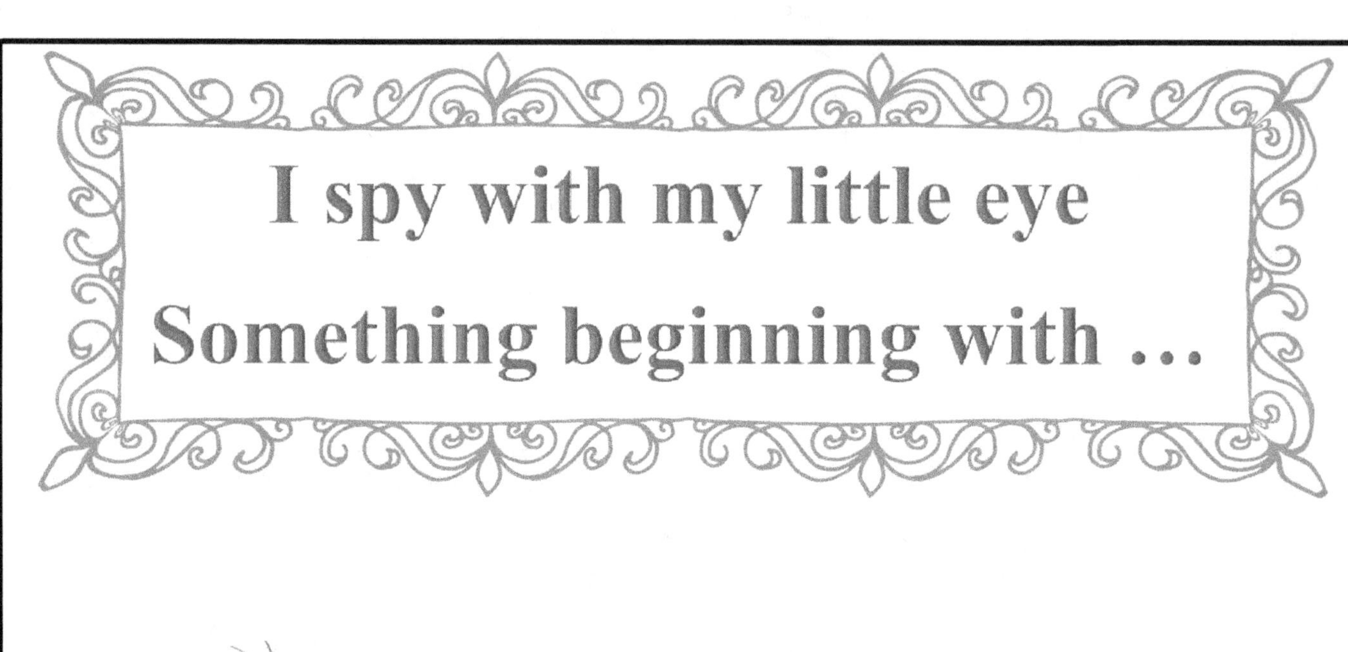

J

It's a

Jam

I spy with my little eye
Something beginning with …

It's a

Kid

I spy with my little eye
Something beginning with ...

L

It's a

Leaf

I spy with my little eye

Something beginning with …

It's

Maize

I spy with my little eye

Something beginning with ...

N

It's

Nuts

I spy with my little eye
Something beginning with …

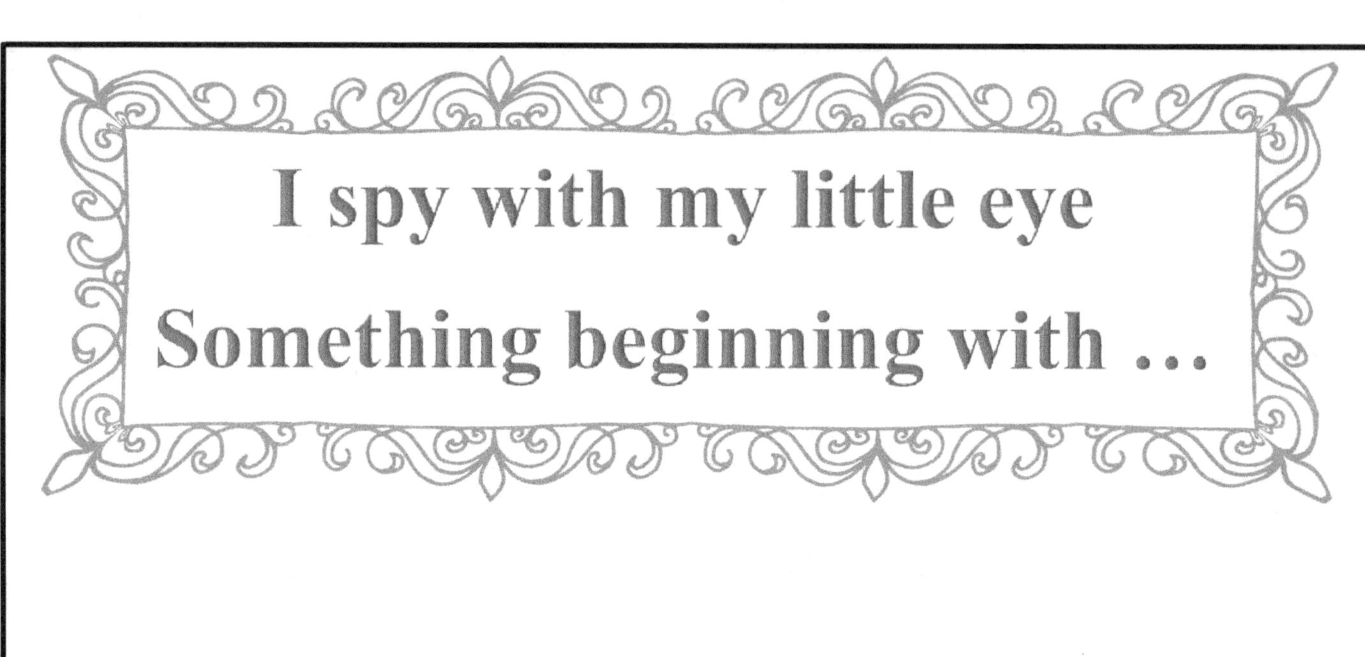

It's an

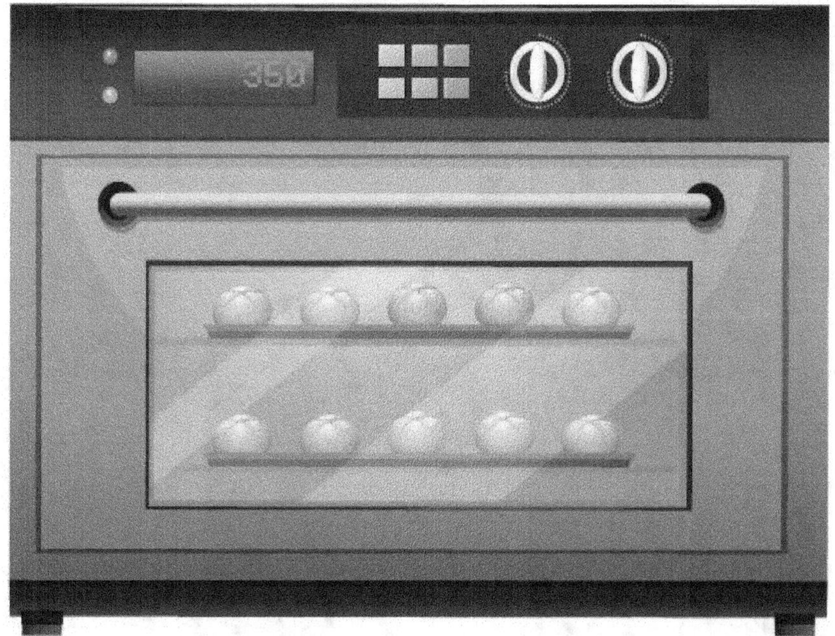

Oven

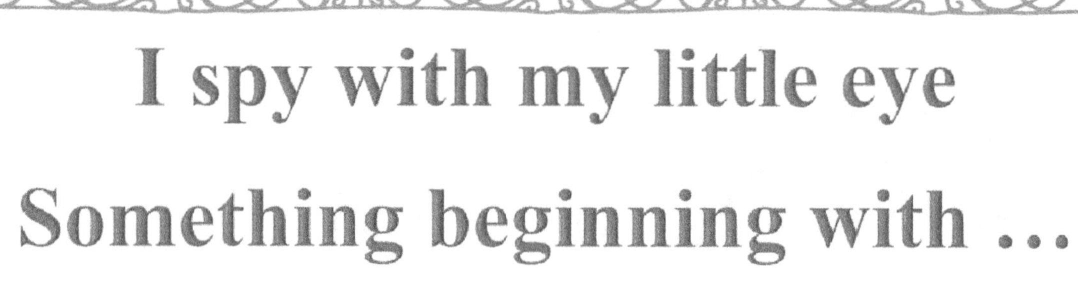

P

It's a

Pumpkin

I spy with my little eye
Something beginning with …

It's a

Quince

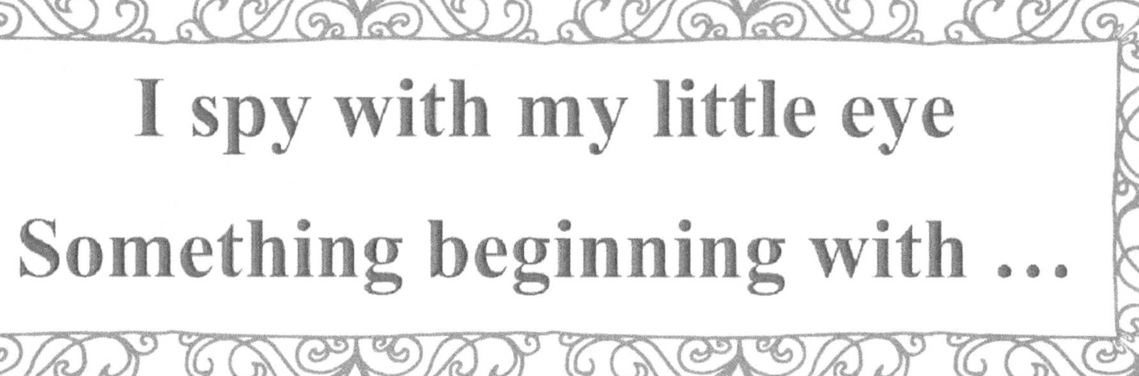

R

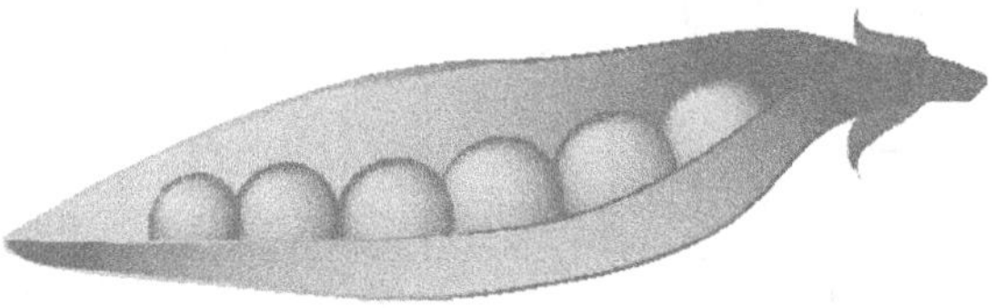

It's a

Raven

I spy with my little eye
Something beginning with …

It's a

Squirrel

I spy with my little eye
Something beginning with …
T

It's a

Turkey

I spy with my little eye
Something beginning with …

It's a

Unicorn

I spy with my little eye
Something beginning with …

It's a

Vanilla

I spy with my little eye
Something beginning with …

W

It's a

W inter

I spy with my little eye
Something beginning with ...

It's an

Xray Fish

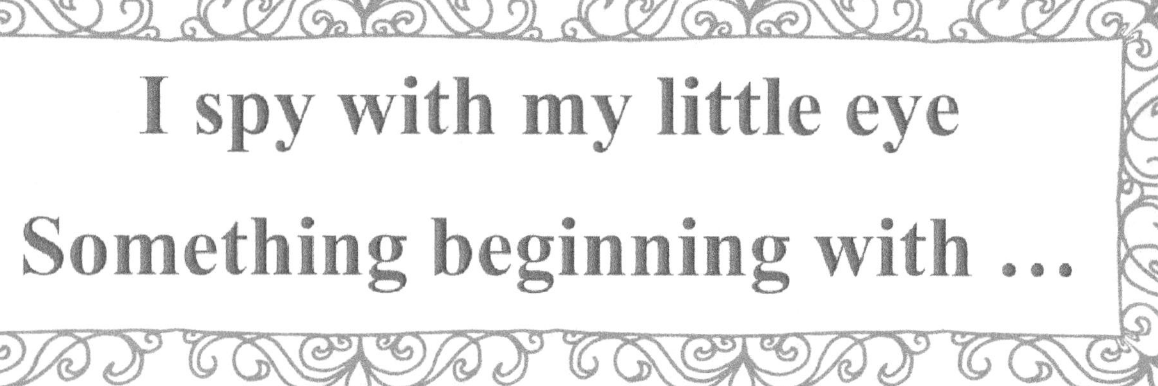

I spy with my little eye
Something beginning with …

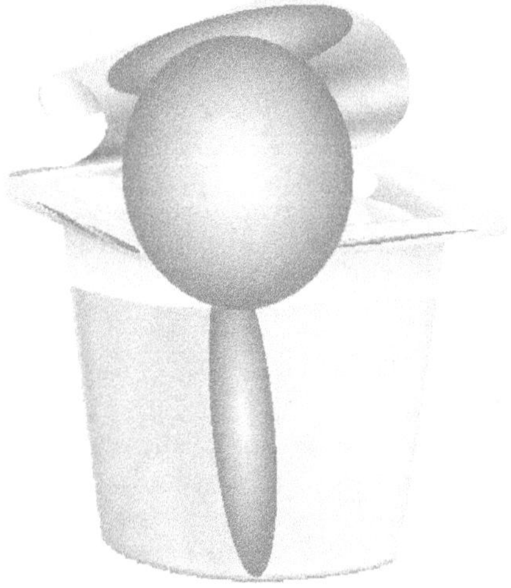

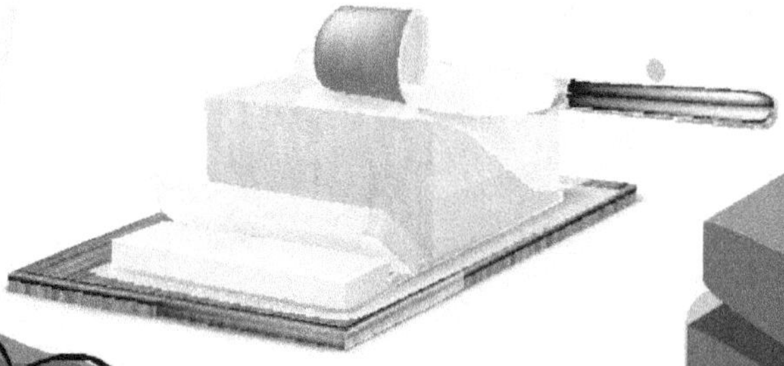

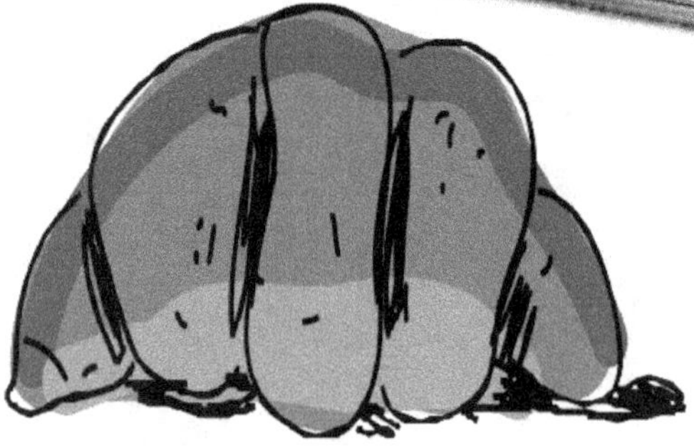

It's a

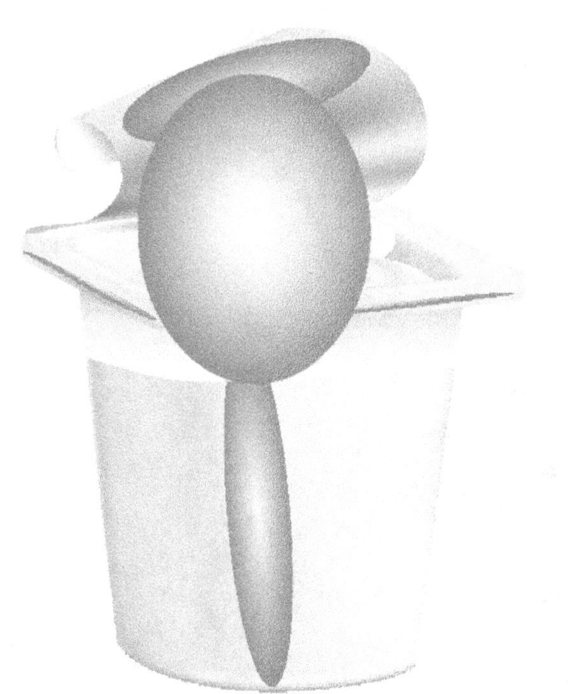

Yoghurt

I spy with my little eye
Something beginning with …
Z

It's a

Zucchini

www.ingramcontent.com/pod-product-compliance
Lightning Source LLC
Chambersburg PA
CBHW080727120726
48001CB00010B/3165